BHAGWAT GEETA QUOTES FOR LIFE

JOURNEY TOWARDS DISCOVERING YOURSELF

ASHISH KANDWAL

Made with ♥ on the Notion Press Platform
www.notionpress.com

May its teachings illuminate your path, Inspire your soul, and bring you inner peace

Contents

Contents

Contents

Contents

Contents

Preface

"

The Bhagavad Gita, often referred to as the Gita, is not merely a book; it is a spiritual and philosophical masterpiece that has transcended centuries and cultures, providing wisdom and guidance to countless souls on their paths to self-discovery and enlightenment."

ONE

Hare Krishna Hare Rama

"You have the right to work, but never to the fruit of work."

TWO

Hare Krishna Hare Rama

"The soul is neither born and nor does it die."

THREE

Hare Krishna Hare Rama

"I am seated in the hearts of all living beings, and from me come memory, knowledge, and understanding."

FOUR

Hare Krishna Hare Rama

Because the fool wants to become God, He never finds him. The master is already God, Without ever wishing to be.

FIVE

Hare Krishna Hare Rama

"Happiness is a state of mind that has nothing to do with the external world."

SIX

Hare Krishna Hare Rama

"Whatever celestial form a devotee seeks to worship with faith, I steady the faith of such a devotee in that form."

SEVEN

Hare Krishna Hare Rama

Abandon all the attachment to the result of action and attain supreme peace.

EIGHT

Hare Krishna Hare Rama

"When a person responds to the joys and sorrows of others as if they were his own, he has attained the highest state of spiritual union."

NINE

Hare Krishna Hare Rama

"When you fall in love then your heart should fill with happiness, that does not come unless you surrender yourself completely."

TEN

Hare Krishna Hare Rama

"I regard as great even the smallest gift offered by my devotees in pure love, but even great offerings presented by non-devotees do not please me."

ELEVEN

Hare Krishna Hare Rama

"There is neither this world nor the world beyond nor happiness for the one who doubts."

TWELVE

Hare Krishna Hare Rama

"Life without lord Krishna seems like prayers without devotion, words without emotion, followers without fragrance, echo without resonance, existence without a goal, world without soul."

THIRTEEN

Hare Krishna Hare Rama

"Whatever happened, happened for the good. Whatever is happening, is happening for the good. Whatever will happen, will also happen for the good."

FOURTEEN

Hare Krishna Hare Rama

"The body is a temporary vehicle. Without the soul, the body is like a car without a driver."

FIFTEEN

Hare Krishna Hare Rama

"The brightness of the sun, which lights up the world, the brightness of the moon and of fire – these are my glory."

SIXTEEN

Hare Krishna Hare Rama

"Do everything you have to do, but not with ego, not with lust, not with envy but with love, compassion, humility, and devotion."

SEVENTEEN

Hare Krishna Hare Rama

"Change is the law of the universe. You can be a millionaire, or a pauper in an instant."

EIGHTEEN

Hare Krishna Hare Rama

"Blessed is a human birth, even the dwellers in heaven desire this birth, for true knowledge and pure love may be attained only by a human being"

NINETEEN

Hare Krishna Hare Rama

"Everything is unreal. Conquer your mind, and you can conquer the world."

TWENTY

Hare Krishna Hare Rama

"The pleasure from the senses seems like nectar at first, but it is sour as the toxin in the end."

TWENTY-ONE

Hare Krishna Hare Rama

"Change is the law of the world. In a moment you become the owner of millions, in the other you become penniless."

TWENTY-TWO

Hare Krishna Hare Rama

"Never consider yourself the cause of the results of your activities, and never be attached to not doing your duty."

TWENTY-THREE

Hare Krishna Hare Rama

"From passion comes the confusion of mind, then the loss of remembrance, the forgetting of duty."

TWENTY-FOUR

Hare Krishna Hare Rama

"Whatever happened was good. What's happening is going well. Whatever will happen, will also be good. Do not worry about the future live in present."

TWENTY-FIVE

Hare Krishna Hare Rama

"For one who has conquered his mind, a mind is best of friends, but for one who has failed to do so, a mind is the greatest enemy."

TWENTY-SIX

Hare Krishna Hare Rama

"As a strong wind sweeps away a boat on the water, even one of the roaming senses on which the mind focusses can carry away a man's intelligence."

TWENTY-SEVEN

Hare Krishna Hare Rama

"I have a purpose for your pain, a reason for your struggle, and a reward for your faithfulness. Trust me and don't give up."

TWENTY-EIGHT

Hare Krishna Hare Rama

The Gift is Pure When it is Given from the Heart to the Right Person at the Right time & the Right place, and we expect nothing in return.

TWENTY-NINE

Hare Krishna Hare Rama

"The wise should work without attachment, for the welfare of society."

THIRTY

Hare Krishna Hare Rama

"Works do not bind Me, because I have no desire for the fruits of work."

THIRTY-ONE

Hare Krishna Hare Rama

"There is nothing, animate or inanimate, that can exist without Me."

THIRTY-TWO

Hare Krishna Hare Rama

"When meditation is mastered, The mind is unwavering like the flame of a lamp in a windless place."

THIRTY-THREE

Hare Krishna Hare Rama

"Calmness, gentleness, silence, self-restraint, purity: these are the disciplines of the mind."

THIRTY-FOUR

Hare Krishna Hare Rama

"The meaning of love can be seen in the mother's eyes."

THIRTY-FIVE

Hare Krishna Hare Rama

"Man is made by his belief. As he believes, so he is."

THIRTY-SIX

Hare Krishna Hare Rama

"Death is certain for one who has been born, and rebirth is inevitable for one who has died. Therefore, you should not Lament over the Inevitable."

THIRTY-SEVEN

Hare Krishna Hare Rama

"I want to forget you but then realize that moving on also means accepting that some memories will stay forever."

THIRTY-EIGHT

Hare Krishna Hare Rama

"A person can rise through the efforts of his own mind; in fact, he alone is the sculptor of his own destiny."

THIRTY-NINE

Hare Krishna Hare Rama

"No one becomes a karma yogi who has not renounced the selfish motive behind an action."

FORTY

HareKrishna Hare Rama

"As you put on fresh new clothes and take off those you've worn, You'll replace your body with a fresh one, newly born."

FORTY-ONE

Hare Krishna Hare Rama

"Why do you worry unnecessarily? Whom do you fear? Who can kill you? The soul is neither born nor dies."

FORTY-TWO

Hare Krishna Hare Rama

"Hell has three gates: lust, anger and greed."

FORTY-THREE

Hare Krishna Hare Rama

"Listen to your heart and take decisions, don't be confused by other advice, your heart voice is my voice."

FORTY-FOUR

Hare Krishna Hare Rama

"Because everything is born of me, I am the original source of all. Everything is under me, no one is above me."

FORTY-FIVE

Hare Krishna Hare Rama

"The fire of knowledge burns all karmas to ashes."

FORTY-SIX

Hare Krishna Hare Rama

"If you think he is not answering your prayers just remember he feels your pain."

FORTY-SEVEN

Hare Krishna Hare Rama

"All works are being done by the energy and power of nature, but due to the delusion of ego people assume themselves to be the doer."

FORTY-EIGHT

Hare Krishna Hare Rama

"Don't misunderstand everything be calm and thinks logically it's your suspicious mind that disturbing you not others."

FORTY-NINE

Hare Krishna Hare Rama

Somebody somewhere is depending on you do to what God has called you to do.

FIFTY

Hare Krishna Hare Rama

"Don't look to anyone for your needs. For the one who created you, waters you."

FIFTY-ONE

Hare Krishna Hare Rama

"Reshape yourself through the power of your will never let yourself be degraded by self-will. The will is the only friend of the Self, and the will is the only enemy of the Self."

FIFTY-TWO

Hare Krishna Hare Rama

"Whenever you feel unloved, unimportant or insecure, remember to whom you belong."

FIFTY-THREE

Hare Krishna Hare Rama

"No one should abandon duties because he sees defects in them, Every action, every activity is surrounded by defects as a fire is surrounded by smoke."

FIFTY-FOUR

Hare Krishna Hare Rama

"There are two primary choices in life to accept conditions as they exist or accept responsibility for changing them."

FIFTY-FIVE

Hare Krishna Hare Rama

"Death is as sure for that which is born, as birth is for that which is dead. Therefore grieve not for what is inevitable."

FIFTY-SIX

Hare Krishna Hare Rama

"Selflessness is the only way to progress and prosperity."

FIFTY-SEVEN

Hare Krishna Hare Rama

"Wrong thinking is the only problem in life."

FIFTY-EIGHT

Hare Krishna Hare Rama

"I look upon all creatures equally; none are less dear to me and none dearer. But those who worship me with love live in me, and I come to life in them."

FIFTY-NINE

Hare Krishna Hare Rama

"Whatever the state of being that a man may focus upon at the end, when he leaves his body, to that state of being he will go."

SIXTY

Hare Krishna Hare Rama

"Perform all thy actions with mind concentrated on the Divine, renouncing attachment and looking upon success and failure with an equal eye. Spirituality implies equanimity."

SIXTY-ONE

Hare Krishna Hare Ram

"You came empty-handed, and you will leave empty-handed."

SIXTY-TWO

Hare Krishna Hare Rama

"It is better to live your own destiny imperfectly than to live an imitation of somebody else's life with perfection."

SIXTY-THREE

Hare Krishna Hare Rama

"Arise, slay thy enemies, enjoy a prosperous kingdom."

SIXTY-FOUR

Hare Krishna Hare Rama

"Develop the right attitude towards your job and even the most mundane work becomes a source of joy."

SIXTY-FIVE

Hare Krishna Hare Rama

"He who has no attachments can really love others, for his love is pure and divine."

SIXTY-SIX

Hare Krishna Hare Rama

"The real sign of weakness in anyone is yielding to dualities & running away from their overriding duty of the moment."

SIXTY-SEVEN

Hare Krishna Hare Rama

"Creation is only the projection into the form of that which already exists."

SIXTY-EIGHT

Hare Krishna Hare Rama

"Perform your obligatory duty, because the action is indeed better than inaction."

SIXTY-NINE

Hare Krishna Hare Rama

"God does not involve himself in the sinful or virtuous deeds of anyone. the living entities are deluded because their inner knowledge is covered by ignorance."

SEVENTY

Hare Krishna Hare Rama

"Dissolves bad habits, evil thoughts & Negative emotions."

SEVENTY-ONE

Hare Krishna Hare Rama

"Live your life the way you want, don't be a slave to others wishes."

SEVENTY-TWO

Hare Krishna Hare Rama

"Don't be proud of what you have, you can't bring your belongings with your coffin."

SEVENTY-THREE

Hare Krishna Hare Rama

"Good work is never wasted, always rewarded by God."

SEVENTY-FOUR

Hare Krishna Hare Rama

"There are three gates to self-destruction and hell
Lust, Anger & Greed."

SEVENTY-FIVE

Hare Krishna Hare Rama

"Among all kinds of killers, time is the ultimate because time kills everything."

SEVENTY-SIX

Hare Krishna Hare Rama

"Always follow your inner self and do what it says."

SEVENTY-SEVEN

Hare Krishna Hare Rama

The soul can never be cut to pieces by any weapon, nor burned by fire, nor moistened by water, nor withered by the wind.

SEVENTY-EIGHT

Hare Krishna Hare Rama

"Seek refuge in the attitude of detachment and you will amass the wealth of spiritual awareness."

SEVENTY-NINE

Hare Krishna Hare Rama

"I want to forget you but then realize that moving on also means accepting that some memories will stay forever."

EIGHTY

Hare Krishna Hare Rama

"The consciousness of the individual soul is prone to be forgetful but the consciousness of the Supreme is all knowledge."

EIGHTY-ONE

Hare Krishna Hare Rama

"If you perform the sacrifice of doing your duty, you do not have to do anything else. Devoted to duty, man attains perfection."

EIGHTY-TWO

Hare Krishna Hare Rama

"Fear not. What is not real, Never was and never will be. What's true, Always was and cannot be destroyed."

EIGHTY-THREE

Hare Krishna Hare Rama

"A man is made by his beliefs. As he believes. So He becomes."

EIGHTY-FOUR

Hare Krishna Hare Rama

"The mind acts like an enemy for those who do not control it."

EIGHTY-FIVE

Hare Krishna Hare Rama

"Delusion arises from anger. The mind is bewildered by delusion"

EIGHTY-SIX

Hare Krishna Hare Rama

"No one that does good work will ever come to a terrible ending, either in the world to come."

EIGHTY-SEVEN

Hare Krishna Hare Rama

Time is the beginning & the end.

EIGHTY-EIGHT

Hare Krishna Hare Rama

"I didn't know what I was looking for, but I knew whatever it was that I was looking for was real."

EIGHTY-NINE

Hare Krishna Hare Rama

"Failure is when you accept it, otherwise, it's just another obstacle."

NINETY

Hare Krishna Hare Rama

"The only way you can conquer me is through love and there I am gladly conquered."

NINETY-ONE

Hare Krishna Hare Rama

"Man is the slave of money, but money is no man's slave."

NINETY-TWO

Hare Krishna Hare Rama

"Fire turns firewood to ash. Self-knowledge turns to ash all actions of dualities on your mind and brings you inner peace."

NINETY-THREE

Hare Krishna Hare Rama

"As the air carries fragrance from place to place, so does the embodied soul carry the mind and senses with it, when it leaves an old body and enters a new one."

NINETY-FOUR

Hare Krishna Hare Rama

"It is much better to execute one's own duties imperfectly than to learn the responsibilities of another."

NINETY-FIVE

Hare Krishna Hare Rama

"Refusing to yield to dualities is your sacred duty. Do it stay unmoved by them. Or your mind will be in constant turmoil."

NINETY-SIX

Hare Krishna Hare Rama

"They alone see truly who see that the lord the exact same time in every creature."

NINETY-SEVEN

Hare Krishna Hare Rama

"As a mirror is obscured by dust, so the intellect is obscured by anger."

NINETY-EIGHT

Hare Krishna Hare Rama

"If you want to see the brave, look at those who can forgive."

NINETY-NINE

Enter Caption

Those whose minds are established inequality of vision conquer the cycle of birth and death in this very life. they possess the flawless qualities of god and are therefore seated in the absolute truth.

ONE HUNDRED

Hare Krishna Hare Rama

"The soul is neither born and nor does it die."

www.ingramcontent.com/pod-product-compliance
Lightning Source LLC
LaVergne TN
LVHW091111150826
845673LV00002B/776

9798891331921